Kids' Travel Guide
France

FlyingKids Presents:

Kids' Travel Guide
France

Writer: **Shira Halperin**

Editor: **Yael** Ornan

Designer: Keren **Amram**

Cover Designer: Francesca Guido

Illustrator: **Liat Aluf**

Translator: Oren Amir

Translation editor: Yael Valier

Photographs: **Shira** Halperin, **Hadar** Ben Gal

Visit us: www.theflyingkids.com

Contact us: leonardo@theflyingkids.com

ISBN: 978-1499393354

Production:

Notssa
www.notssa.com

Table of Contents

This is the only page for parents in this book…

Dear parents,

If you bought this book, you're probably planning a family trip with your kids. You are spending a lot of time and money in the hopes that this family vacation will be pleasant and fun. You would like your children to learn a little about the country you visit - its geography, history, unique culture, traditions, and more. And you hope they will always remember the trip as a very special experience.

The reality is often quite different. Parents find themselves frustrated as they struggle to convince their kids to join a tour or visit a landmark, while the kids just want to stay in and watch TV. On the road, the children are glued to their mobile devices instead of enjoying the new sights and scenery - or they complain and constantly ask, "When are we going to get there?" Many parents are disappointed after they return home and discover that their kids don't remember much about the trip and the new things they learned.

That's exactly why **Kids' Travel Guide - France** was created. With **Kids' Travel Guide - France**, young children become researchers and active participants in the trip. They learn fun facts about history and culture; they play games and take quizzes. This helps kids - and parents - enjoy the trip a lot more!

A family trip is fun. But difficulties can arise when children are not in their natural environment. **Kids' Travel Guide - France**, takes this into account and supports children as they get ready for the trip, visit new places, learn new things, and finally, return home.

The **Kids' Travel Guide - France**, does this by helping children to prepare for the trip and know what to expect. During the trip, kids will read relevant facts about the United States and get advice on how to adapt to new situations. **Kids' Travel Guide - France**, includes puzzles, tasks to complete, useful tips, and other recommendations along the way. All of this encourages children to experiment, explore, and be more involved in the family's activities - as well as to learn new information and make memories throughout the trip. In addition, kids are asked to document and write about their experiences during the trip, so that when you return home, they will have a memoir that will be fun to look at and reread again and again.

Kids' Travel Guide - France offers general information about France, so it is useful regardless of the city or part of the country you plan to visit. It includes basic geography; flags, symbols and coins; basic history; and colorful facts about culture and customs in the United States.

If you are traveling to the US, you may also want to get the cities series: San Francisco,

Are you ready for a new experience?

HAVE A PLEASANT TRIP!

Hi Kids,

If you are reading this book, it means you are lucky –
You are going to **France**!

You probably know already where you are going, and you may have noticed that your parents are getting ready for the journey. They have bought travel guides, looked for information on the Internet and printed pages of information. They are talking to friends and people who have already visited that place in order to learn about it and know what to do, where to go and when...

This book is not just another guide book for your parents.
But this book is for you only – for the young travelers.

So what is this book all about?

First and foremost, meet **Leonardo**, your very own personal guide on this trip. Leonardo has visited **many places** around the world (Guess how he got there? 😊) and he will be with you throughout the book and the trip until you return home. Leonardo will tell you all about the places you will visit - it is always good to know where you are going, and to learn a little bit about the place and its history beforehand - and will provide many ideas, quizzes, tips and **other surprises.** Leonardo will accompany you while you are packing and leaving home. He will stay in the hotel with you (don't worry, it does not cost more money 😉) and will visit the **sites** with you until you return home and paste the pictures in the right pages, turning it into a wonderful book of memories.

A Travel Diary –The Beginning!
Going to France!!!

How did you get to France?

By plane / train / car / other _____

Date of arrival _____ Time _____ Date of departure _____

All in all ,we will stay in Paris for _____ days

Is this your first visit _____ ?

Where will you sleep? hotel / campsite / apartment / with family / other _____

What sites are you planning on visiting?

_____
_____
_____

What special activities are you planning on doing?

_____
_____
_____

Are you excited about the trip?
This is an excitement indicator. Ask each family member how excited he or she is (from "not at all" up to "very, very much"), and mark it down on the indicator. Leonardo had also marked the level of his excitement…

not at all   very, very much

Leonardo

Who is traveling?

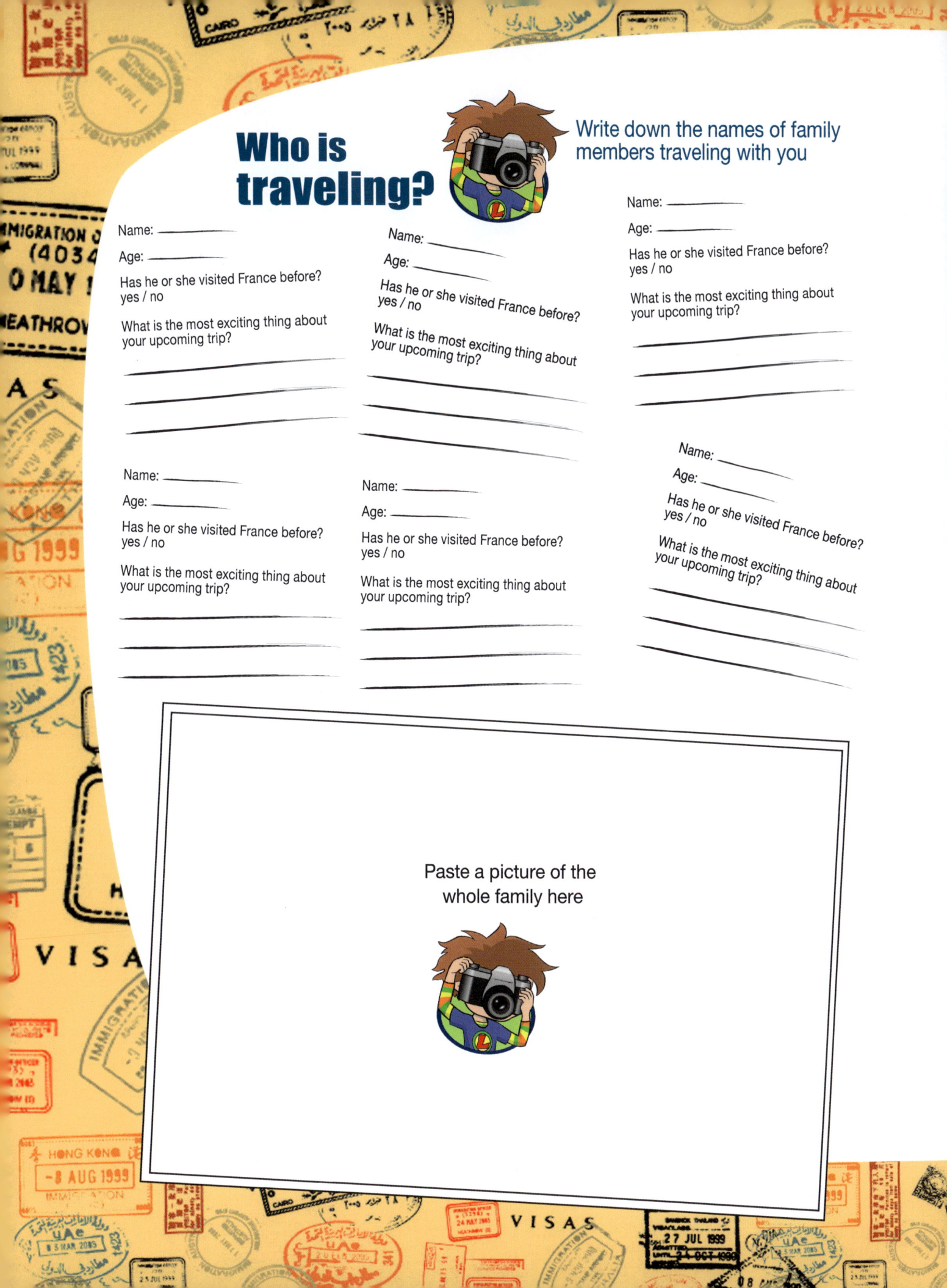

Write down the names of family members traveling with you

Name: ―――――――

Age: ―――――――

Has he or she visited France before?
yes / no

What is the most exciting thing about
your upcoming trip?

―――――――――――――――

―――――――――――――――

―――――――――――――――

Name: ―――――――

Age: ―――――――

Has he or she visited France before?
yes / no

What is the most exciting thing about
your upcoming trip?

―――――――――――――――

―――――――――――――――

―――――――――――――――

Name: ―――――――

Age: ―――――――

Has he or she visited France before?
yes / no

What is the most exciting thing about
your upcoming trip?

―――――――――――――――

―――――――――――――――

Name: ―――――――

Age: ―――――――

Has he or she visited France before?
yes / no

What is the most exciting thing about
your upcoming trip?

―――――――――――――――

―――――――――――――――

Name: ―――――――

Age: ―――――――

Has he or she visited France before?
yes / no

What is the most exciting thing about
your upcoming trip?

―――――――――――――――

―――――――――――――――

Name: ―――――――

Age: ―――――――

Has he or she visited France before?
yes / no

What is the most exciting thing about
your upcoming trip?

―――――――――――――――

―――――――――――――――

Paste a picture of the
whole family here

Preparations at home – do not forget...!

Mom or Dad will take care of packing clothes (how many pairs of pants, which comb to take…). We will only refer to the stuff we think you should think of taking along on your trip to France.

You are going on vacation away from home, Leonardo therefore recommends you take the following:

- Kids' Travel Guide - France - of course!
- comfortable walking shoes
- a rain coat (preferably folded, sometimes it rains without warning)
- a hat (and sunglasses, if you want)
- writing implements
- crayons and pens (It is always nice to color and draw)
- a book
- your smart phone/tablet

Pack a few things for the flight in a small bag (or backpack), such as:

- snacks, fruit, candy and chewing gum. It may help a lot during take off and landing, when there's pressure in your ears.
- Games you can play while sitting down: electronic games, booklets of crossword-puzzles, connect-the-numbers (or connect the dots) etc. Make sure to take a notebook or a writing-pad, pencil and crayons. You can use them for games, for writing, to draw or doodle when you are bored…
- And do not forget to take with the **"Kids' Travel Guide - France"** with you.

Now let's see if you can find 12 items one should take on a trip in this Word Search Puzzle:

P	A	T	I	E	N	C	E	A	W	F	G
E	L	R	T	S	G	Y	J	W	A	T	O
Q	E	Y	U	Y	K	Z	K	M	L	W	O
H	O	S	N	A	S	N	Y	S	K	G	D
A	N	R	Z	C	P	E	N	C	I	L	M
C	A	M	E	R	A	A	W	G	N	E	O
R	R	A	I	N	C	O	A	T	G	Q	O
Y	D	S	G	I	R	K	Z	K	S	H	D
S	O	A	C	O	A	E	T	K	H	A	T
F	R	U	I	T	Y	Q	O	V	O	D	A
B	O	O	K	F	O	H	Z	K	E	R	T
T	K	Z	K	A	N	S	I	E	S	Y	U
O	V	I	E	S	S	N	A	C	K	S	P

Leonardo, walking shoes, hat, rain coat, crayons, book, pencil, camera, snacks, fruit, patience, good mood

La France

France is one of the most beautiful countries in the world, and millions of people arrive there every year to enjoy its wonders: a rich **culture**, a fascinating history, **lovely cities**, great beaches, splendid **lakes**, exciting **ski** resorts and **excellent food**.

Who knows on which continent France is?

(Answer on the next page)

This is a map of the world. Can you point out France?

Go over France's borders and mark them down. Find your home country on the map and follow the aircraft's route from there to France.

Where is France?

France
on the world map

You may have noticed that France is located in the western part of Europe

France is the third largest country in Europe. Only Russia and Ukraine are bigger

What is a compass rose?

A compass rose is a design on a map that shows directions:
North – South – East – West.
Since North is always marked on maps, one can always figure out the other directions.
When going on field trips, one can always use a compass. A compass rose is drawn on the face of the compass and the hand always points to the north.
Knowing where each direction lies helps one navigate and find out where certain places are or how to get from one point to another.

Mark the three missing directions in the blank squares.

North

France is surrounded by many neighboring countries. Can you find them on the map? If so, complete the following:

To the South -_____ and_____

To the East - _____,_____ , and_____

To the North -_____

Borders

Did you know?

In order to differentiate between countries, borders were invented. A border is a line which marks the end of one country's territory and the beginning of another. There are all kinds of borders; sometimes a river or a range of mountains are a natural border, sometimes there is a need to erect a fence or a special gate to mark a border.

In France, for example, there's a natural border to the east: the French Alps (read about them later on), mountains that stretch between France, Italy and Switzerland.

France is also surrounded by seas.
Can you find out their names?

To the south-east _____

To the west _____

Quiz! What is the capital of France?

a. London

b. Elysees

c. Paris

d. The French Riviera

In the Southeast - The Mediterranean
In the West - The Atlantic ocean

Do only French people live in France?

The majority of the people living in France are French (92% of its citizens), but there are also many immigrants from North Africa and Germany.

Immigrants are people who moved permanently to a country which is not their native country.

Do people in France speak French?

Of course they do. Most of the French people speak French, but if you listen carefully, you'll be able to hear other languages spoken as well. Most of these languages, such as Flemish, Alsatian, Breton, Basque and Catalan, are not well known.

You are about to visit wonderful **Paris**, but there are other beautiful cities in France worth visiting.
Use the map to find **15 more lovely French cities** in the following Word Search Puzzle.

A	S	C	H	E	R	B	O	U	R	G	H	I	K	Z
M	F	H	T	J	K	N	T	O	U	L	U	O	S	E
A	V	U	A	S	A	G	Z	N	Q	E	R	V	N	B
R	E	I	O	K	Z	T	O	A	I	L	H	E	L	E
S	L	P	R	R	J	R	E	N	M	C	J	I	I	H
E	G	B	L	I	L	L	E	T	Q	E	E	W	M	N
I	R	Y	E	M	G	K	L	E	E	Y	T	U	O	G
L	E	P	A	R	I	S	W	S	C	S	D	K	G	B
L	N	I	N	O	G	D	N	T	X	H	I	N	E	O
E	O	K	S	U	G	V	V	K	C	B	J	V	S	R
A	B	P	O	E	F	X	T	W	Q	A	O	Z	F	D
Q	L	Y	O	N	I	B	R	E	S	T	N	J	T	E
D	E	E	B	N	K	L	P	S	X	C	B	Y	T	A
D	T	M	O	N	T	E	C	A	R	L	O	G	E	U
J	I	R	F	G	H	K	O	C	A	M	U	J	M	X

paris, monte carlo, bordeaux, orleans, rouen, toulouse, nice, marseille nantes, lille, cherbourg, lyon, dijon, brest, limoges grenoble

What other beautiful tourist attraction and sites are there in France?

The French Alps' beauty is overwhelming. The region is rich with high mountains, valleys, sparkling **lakes** and **rivers**. Its beauty attracts many tourists from all over the world. In winter, one can go **skiing** on the snowy mountain slopes, and in summer **enjoy the scenic drives in nature.**

What is a valley? A lowland surrounded by mountains or hills.

The French Riviera is a resort area, famous in France and worldwide. In French, the Riviera is called La Côte D'Azure, meaning "sky-blue coast". There are small, resort villages in the Riviera, beautiful cities such as Marseille, Cannes and Monaco, and naturally, some splendid and exotic beaches. It is said that the residents of this region are not at all like the typical French people; they are much more **relaxed** and calm (no wonder… 😉). The rich and the famous love to spend time in the French Riviera, and you may be lucky enough to see a **famous movie star** driving by in a fancy car…

Flags, symbols and coins

This is the **flag** of **France**.
The French call it Le Tricolor. If you don't know what Tricolor means, take a look at the flag and try to figure it out by looking at the number of its colors ('tri' means three) 😉 .

Did you know?

In the past, each stripe was of a different width. It was Napoleon who decided that the stripes should be of the same width size and he changed the flag, although the French army still uses the old one.

This is the symbol of France. If you take a close look, you can see that there are two kinds of leaves: olive leaves, which symbolize peace, and oak leaves which stand for eternity because the oak is a very strong tree. The axe is justice while the letters RF are the first initials of the words, the "French Republic," or, as the French say: La Republique Francaise.

If you want to buy something in France, how do you pay for it?

Up until a few years ago, the French had their own currency, the Franc. In 1999, the **Franc** was replaced by the European currency named the **Euro**.

The French Alps

The European Union (EU)

The European Union is a federation of 27 countries in Europe. Each is an independent state, but they all have some common characteristics, the currency being one of them. If you visit Spain, Germany or France, you will use the Euro although each of these countries is independent and stands on its own.

And this is the Euro

This is the French Franc

Did you know?

If the European Union were one big country (like the United States of America, which is comprised of 50 states), it would have been the third largest country in the world.

The flag of the European Union

Once, many years ago...

Have you ever heard of the French Revolution? Or maybe the name Napoleon rings a bell? 😊 The history of France is fascinating.

People have lived in the area which is now called France as far back as the Stone Age, but then it was not called, "France," of course. As in all countries which have been in existence for many years, France was ruled throughout the ages by kings, tyrants* and sovereigns. For over 130 years, it has been headed by presidents. Let us try to put things in order so that we can understand France's history.

*a tyrant – an evil ruler

In ancient times, the area was called **Gaul** and it was inhabited by the Gallic tribes. Julius Caesar conquered Gaul and annexed it to the Roman Empire. In the 6th century, more than 1,400 years ago, Gaul was overrun by Germanic tribes, the "Franks" led by King Karl the Great, who conquered France as well as large areas of **Europe**. Although it was a powerful, vaste empire, it did not last long. During the reign of **Karl the Great's** grand-children, the empire was divided and its **western part** became a separate kingdom, known today as **France.**

Through the years, many kings ruled the kingdom, but around 1,000 CE, one dynasty of kings came to power and ruled France for 800 years.

Karl the Great

*Dynasty – a succession of rulers from the same family. The king's son is the heir to the king, he becomes the king and then his son replaces him and so on. Thus the kingship remains in the family.

Did you know?

One of the most famous wars which took place during these years was the **"Hundred Years' War"** between France and England. You are probably guessing that it lasted 100 years... The truth is, it lasted 116 years (from 1337 until 1453)! 😊

Louis the 14ᵗʰ was a famous king, who ruled France from 1661 until 1715. He was the most powerful and well-known king of all European monarchs, and you may read more about him later.

Have you ever heard about the French Revolution?

About 70 years after the reign of Louis the 14ᵗʰ, France was going through a difficult period. The kings who ruled the country were evil and dishonest: they imposed high taxes on the people, disregarding their hardships, and prevented them from getting an education ☹. The kings seized people's lands, wasted money and plunged France into a tough economic situation.

The situation became unbearable until the people united – the peasants, the educated and the workers – and fought against the rule of the kings. A war broke out in 1789, and that is what we call The **French Revolution**. It is an important event in the history of France and that of humanity because at that time, the common people succeeded in revolting and putting an end to the kingship. The kingdom was replaced by a republic – a form of government by the people.

Louis the 14ᵗʰ

Did you know?

Many people in France were so poor that they could not even buy bread to eat, but the nobility did not care. It is said that the royal family was so removed from the common people that when Queen Marie Antoinette heard that the people had no bread, she responded, "Let them eat cake!"

The republican government did not last long and after a short period of chaos, **Napoleon Bonaparte** came to power (you will learn about him later) and declared himself Emperor.

In 1814, France and Germany became bitter enemies and began to fight each other constantly. In 1914, the First World War broke out and France joined the Allies who fought the Germans. France suffered many casualties, but thanks to the assistance of the **American army**, Germany was defeated.

The war cost much money and France's economy lapsed into difficulty. The French people were hungry again.

During World War 2, which broke out in 1939, France once again fought **Germany**, but the strong German army defeated the French and conquered large parts of France. The German occupation lasted about five years until 1944, when the "Allied Forces" landed in Normandy in northern France, the occupied zone was liberated and **France was once again reunited**.

The "Allied Forces" – a military force comprised of soldiers from several countries who fought together against Germany.

At the end of the war, France invested heavily in creating work and financial stability and was slowly rehabilitated.

This is how soliders ones looked

If you want to buy a souvenir in France, what currency will you use?

Euro, of course

Famous leaders and rulers

Let us meet a few of the leaders and rulers who influenced France throughout the years:

Pleased to meet you - King Louis the 14th

King Louis the 14th lived from 1638 to 1715 and was one of the strongest monarchs in the history of France. He used to say
"I am the state" because he thought he was the most **important** person in France and the only one who had the authority to make decisions.

The father of Louis the 14th (King Louis the 13th, of course 😉), died prematurely and young Prince Louis was crowned at the age of five. His mother, Queen Anne, **replaced** him until he grew up and was old enough to sit on the throne.
Louis the 14th was a very **smart king**. He built his palace in Versailles (and not in the capital, Paris), and in doing so succeeded in removing those who tried to undermine him and take over the kingship. He spent the first part of his reign **fighting** his neighbors – Holland, Belgium and Germany. A succession of impressive **victories** helped him strengthen and establish France as a leading country in Europe. But the final years of his reign were difficult and unpleasant for the French people. King Louis conquered Spain, but the cost of the war was high and its **large expenses** led France to an
economic crisis.
Nevertheless, in the history of France, King Louis the 14th is regarded as a prominent and powerful monarch.

Among his impressive achievements are the building of the **Palace of Versailles**, which is considered the finest example of architecture and art in France, and the design of gardens and furniture which still bear his name - "Louis the 14th" style.

King Louis the 14th

Pleased to meet you – Napoleon Bonaparte

Napoleon Bonaparte was France's most significant ruler in the 19th century, and his influence spread all over Europe.

Did you know?

It is thought that Napoleon was a **short** man, but this is not true. The mistake is a result of the difference between the French measurement system and the English one. At his death, Napoleon was slightly **taller** than 5 French feet. The French "foot" was longer than the English one so Napoleon was actually about 1.68 meters tall, which was not considered so short in his time.

Napoleon was a brilliant military commander, known all over Europe for his great victories and many conquests. He was only **24 years old** when he was appointed **general** and commanded the French army. He was famous for his ability to build a **war strategy** that led to victories which nobody thought were possible.

At the age of 35, Napoleon became the **ruler of France**, after the turbulent times of the French Revolution. He succeeded in stabilizing the country and taking care of its citizens. A year and a half after being made the Emperor of the French, he was also crowned King of Italy.

Did you know?

During that period, the pope crowned an emperor, so as to symbolize that the emperor was subject to the Church and the pope. During Napoleon's coronation as Emperor of the French, however, he took the crown from the pope and placed it on his own head, as if to say that he, Napoleon, did not wish to be subordinate to anyone!

Napoleon Bonaparte

Napoleon married **Josephine de Beauharnais**, but they were divorced 13 years later. (It is said that the reason was Josephine's inability to bear children.) Napoleon then married **Marie-Louise of Austria**, daughter of the Emperor of Austria, possibly in order to unite the two nations.

Despite his impressive achievements, Napoleon's end was tragic. His army suffered a great loss in a war against Russia. Out of 500,000 soldiers who went to war, less than 100,000 survived and Napoleon returned to Paris defeated and humiliated. Napoleon's position became unstable. The Allied forces united in order to defeat the French army, conquered Paris, forced Napoleon to leave his office and sent him to exile on the isle of Elba.

A short while later, Napoleon tried to recruit an army of volunteers in order to fight back to secure his position as Emperor. The famous Battle of Waterloo was Napoleon's last battle and he was beaten by the English army. He was driven away from France and exiled to the island of St. Helena, where he spent the rest of his life. **Napoleon died before his 52ⁿᵈ birthday.**

Napoleon left an impressive legacy: imposing **architectural structures** (such as the Arc de Triomphe - the triumphal arch, about which you may read later ....) and a code of advanced laws which did not exist until his time, among them the **Equality Laws** which state that all human beings are born equal and all have a right to acquire property.

Napoleon is remembered also for his brilliant quotes*. Here are some of them:

"An army marches on its stomach."

"You are longer than me, not taller"
This was his answer to a soldier who claimed to be taller than Napoleon.

"If you want a thing done well, do it yourself."

"You can do everything with a spear, except sit on it."

*A quote means to repeat words or a sentence that someone else said."

Pleased to meet you – Charles de Gaulle

Charles de Gaulle was **one of the greatest politicians in the 20th century**. He was born in 1890 and died 80 years later. De Gaulle was a young and **gifted** officer who was known for his ability to thwart German military tactics during **World War 2**, while Germany was trying to invade France and other parts of Europe. Following the German invasion of France, de Gaulle escaped to England and was appointed **prime minister in exile** (a prime minister who runs his country from another place). In 1944, de Gaulle entered Paris at the head of the **Allied Forces,** liberated the city from the Germans and became famous all over the world.

In the late 1940's, De Gaulle opposed the way France was run and retired from military and political life. However, in 1958 he was called back to **head the country** when times were difficult, economically and politically. During his period as **president**, de Gaulle strengthened France's economy and its position in the world and made France a **powerful**, independent country.

Did you know?

About **75 million** visitors go to France annually, much more than the number of tourists who visit Spain or the United States, for example.

Who am I?

- Although I was considered a short man, I am the most famous military figure in the history of France.
- Despite the fact that France suffered economic hardships during my time, I am regarded as its most successful king.
- Thanks to me, France today is a modern and powerful state.

Quizzes!

(1) Napoleon (2) Louis the 14th (3) De Gaulle

We've talked a lot about France, now it is time to discuss the French people…

Culture and customs

Do you know any French people? Have you ever heard the names Jean-Paul, Pierre, Jacques or Marie-Louise? We've talked a lot about France, but what about the French people?

What characterizes the French? What do they like to do in their **spare time?** Where do they work? Which **customs are unique** to France?

⬤ The French appreciate food and like to talk about it. Not only do they enjoy cooking and buying good food, but they also arrange the food on the plate in a special, fine way (there will be a chapter dedicated to French food).

⬤ The French are aesthetic people. Their well-planned streets and avenues, their lovely gardens, their excellent taste in fashion and their stores - which sometimes look like food museums - make it is easy to understand the French admiration for beauty and *aesthetics.

*Aesthetics – a branch of philosophy dealing with the criticism of art, the nature of beauty and the awareness of it.

⬤ Local patriotism – you may have noticed that the French love their culture, especially their language. It seems as if they don't even make an effort to speak or understand other languages. Most of the signs, the menus in the restaurants and tourism booklets are written in French only. Even foreign TV programs - and not only for children - are *dubbed into French!

*Dubbing – voices recorded over that of the actors in a film render the film's dialogue in a different language.

What impression did the French make on you?

1. They are charming

    2. They are quite nice

  3. Not so nice

    4. I cannot make up my mind

Bon appétit! – French cuisine (cooking)

The French are known for their **excellent, tasty dishes.** Most adults will tell you that the French style of cooking is superb (they may use other descriptions, but they all agree that the cuisine is excellent 😉). The French love to eat. They may not eat large quantities of food, but they love to **buy** it, **prepare** it and **talk** about it.

One cannot go to France without knowing certain basic and important facts about French food. The following will give you some idea about what is going on:

Where to eat

● A patisserie

– a bakery of sweet cakes and pastries. The shop windows of the patisseries are so beautiful and yummy that you may want to take their picture. Why not?

Paste a souvenir picture of a patisserie's shop window here.

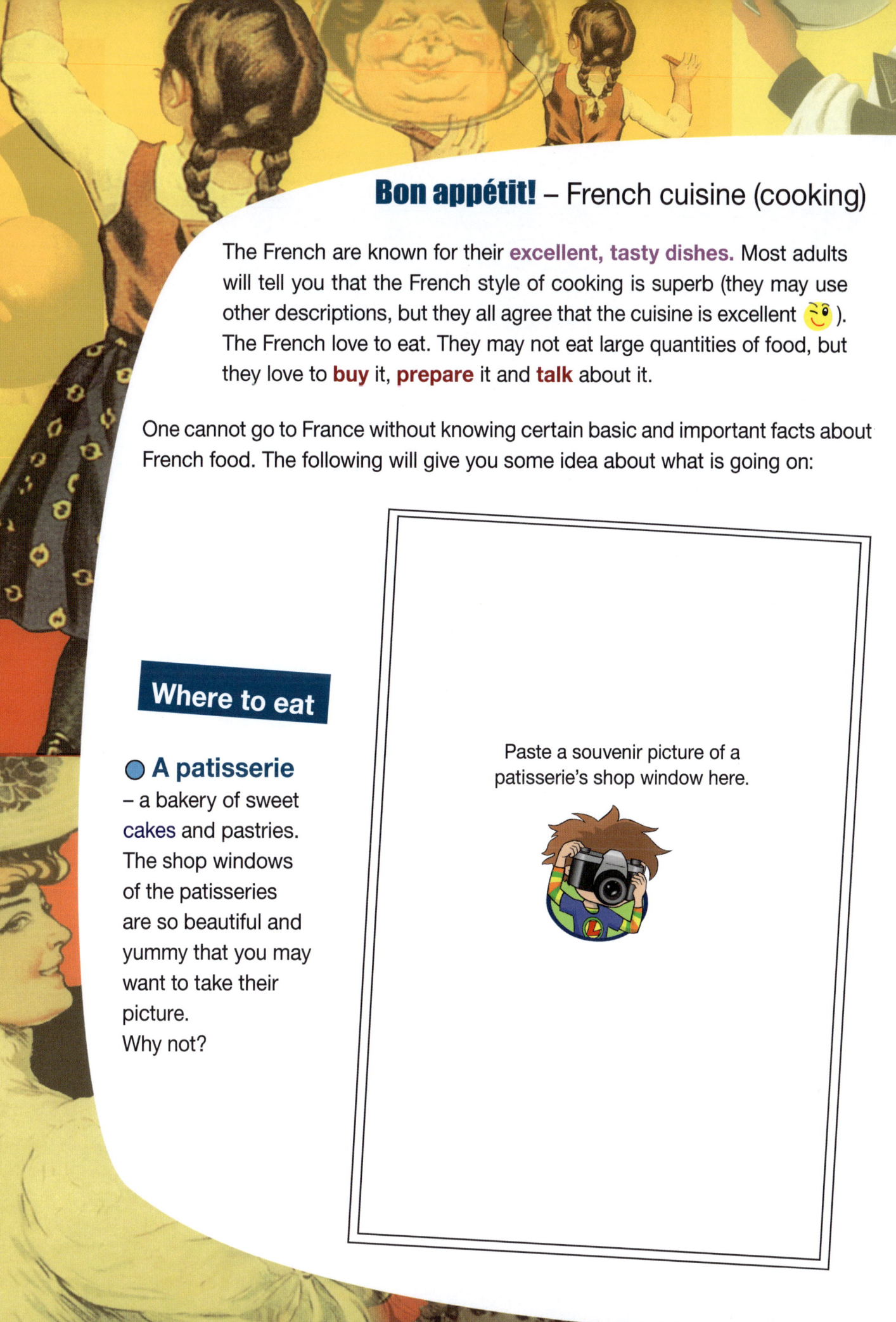

Cremerie – a store for cheese

🔵 **Boulangerie** – a shop for bread and cakes. Some of these shops bake their own pastries in a bakery at the back of the store, and the smell that comes out of there is overwhelming.

🔵 **Cremerie** – a store for cheese. For those of you who like cheese, this is heaven…

🔵 **Café** – when you say "café" in French, it means a coffee shop. Most cafés serve light lunches as well.

🔵 **Brasserie** – a large restaurant serving local food and alcoholic beverages.

🔵 **Bistro** – a small restaurant serving simple meals in a homely setting.

🔵 **Food markets** – there are several food markets in Paris and to visit there is a wonderful experience – the smells, the colors and the variety of groceries are delightful.

Now that we've learned about the places where one can eat, let us get to know some of the tasty dishes one should eat when in Paris. When you sit in a restaurant and look at the menu or stand in line at a patisserie, take a look at the list in the book and find these recommended dishes:

Pastries

If you don't like to try new food (meat or side dishes), ask your parents to order a tasty sandwich. Paris is a paradise for bread lovers and whatever is made of dough and baked in an oven: brioche (a kind of light-textured bread), an éclair (pastry filled with cream and covered in chocolate) and a croissant, of course.

Cheese

France is famous for its variety of **cheese**. It is recommended to taste Camembert, Pont-Leveque and Chevre. The French sour cream, called "crème fraiche," is very tasty.

Meat

If you wish to order chicken, look for the word **"poulet"** in the menu. If you want veal, look for **veau.**

And what about desserts?

The names of traditional French desserts are enough to make your mouth water:
- 🔵 Tart Tatin (an upside-down apple pie)
- 🔵 Profiterole (a small, round cream puff served with ice-cream and hot chocolate sauce)
- 🔵 Flan (baked custard, a sort of pudding)
- 🔵 Crème Brulee (custard topped with a layer of hard caramel)

And how can we do without…
a chocolate mousse!

Pastrie

Leonardo has just landed in France and he already has the urge to try some delicious foods 😉. Help him find them…

Where can he find some good cheese? _____

Where can he find tasty bread? _____

And if he wants something sweet to eat, where would you advise him to go? _____

What new dishes did you see?
More importantly, what new dishes did you taste?

Name of the dish (if you don't know its name, write down what it looks like)	Did you taste it? (yes or no)	Description of dish (what does it include, how does it look)	How do you grade it? (bad, good or excellent

Did you taste a dish that looks exactly like something you eat at home, but tastes different?

_____

_____

Majority rules! **A family vote:**
Which dish was voted as favorite among your family members?

Name	What dish did you like the best?

The winning dish is: _____

How do you say it in French...?
(a handy dictionary)

It is easy to recognize the French language. When you hear it, you know right away what it is. Some French words sound almost the same in English (for example, "dinner" in English and "le dinner" in French) because both languages were derived from Latin.

Do you want to feel a little independent and speak some French? Here are some words that will help you get by. You can practice them later on...

Being polite

Bonjour	Hello/good morning
Bonsoir	Good evening
Au revoir	Bye bye/see you
Oui	Yes
Non	No
S'il vous plait	Please
Merci	Thank you
Merci beaucoup	Thank you very much
De rien	You're welcome
Excusez moi	Excuse me
Pardon	Sorry/pardon me
Je ne parle pas Francais	I do not speak French
Parlez vous Anglais?	Do you speak English?

At the restaurant

Restaurant	Restaurant
Breakfast	Le petit dejeuner
Lunch	Le dejeuner
Dinner	Le dinner
Butter	Du beurre
Bread	Du pain
A cup	Une tasse
A glass	Un verre
Fork	Une fourchette
Knife	Un couteau
Spoon	Une cuillere
Sugar	Du sucre
Wine	Du vin
Salt	Du sel
Pepper	Du poivre
Croissants	Des croissants
Honey	Du miel
Eggs	Des oeufs
An omelette	Une omelette
Snails	Des escargots
Sausage	Du saucisson
Salad	Une salade
Soup	Une soup
Fish	Du poisson
Meat	La viande
Beef	Le Boeuf
Lamb	Le mouton
Pork	Le Pork
Steak	Le Steak
Veal	Le veau
Chicken	Le poulet
Noodles	Les Nouilles
Pasta	Les Pates
Potatoes	Les Pommes de terre
Cheese	Du Fromage
The bill	La note

Competition!
Who remembers more French words?
Ask each other and award points for each correcly remembered word.
Who won?

Need to buy something?

One	Un
Two	Deux
Three	Trois
Four	Quatre
Five	Cinq
Six	Six
Seven	Sept
Eight	Huit
Nine	Neuf
Ten	Dix
One hundred	Cent
One thousand	Mille

Practice a few sentences to help you memorize the words:

● In English – Excuse me, I don't speak French

In French -   Excusez moi, je ne parle pas Francais

● In English – How much is a ticket to the subway (the Metro)?

In French - _____

● In English – Good evening, where is the train station?

In French - _____

● Say your home phone number in French

● Count from 1 to 10 in French

● Say your hotel room number in French

And to sum it all up…

Summary of the trip

We had great fun, what a pity it is over ….

Which places in France did you visit?

_____

Whom did we meet….

● Did you meet tourists from other countries? Yes / no
  If you did meet tourists, where did they come from
  (name their nationalities):

_____

_____

Shopping and souvenirs……..

● What did you buy on the trip?

_____

_____

● What did you want to buy, but ended up not buying?

_____

_____

Grade the most beautiful places and the best experiences of your journey:

First place –

Second place –

Third place –

And now, a difficult task – discuss it with your family and decide

What did you enjoy most on the trip?

Games and Activites

Insert your own words and a funny story will come out

Yesterday morning we drove to _____. We met _____ and _____.
We suggested they join us. They said _____ and went to _____.
When we neared ____, we saw the _____. We were really surprised.
At first, we thought it was _____, but pretty soon we realized that it was _____. _____ said that the best thing would be to _____ and we all agreed.
When we reached the hotel, we decided to _____. Most of us thought it was a bad idea, but in the end, we all agreed. When we started walking towards _____, we found out _____.
That is why we have decided to drop the whole thing. We went back to _____ pretty tired but happy.

Who am I and what is my name (and what do I do...)?

Discover where the tourists are from, what they're wearing and what they are doing on their vacation (Try using the table)

- The three tourists arrived from Israel, America and England
- The tourist wearing the suit drinks tea
- The tourist who drinks tea is not from America or Israel
- The tourist with the pants and shirt didn't drink tea and didn't take any pictures today.
- The tourist from America is resting on the bench.
- The tourist who is taking pictures arrived on a night flight from Israel
- The tourist from England is not wearing jeans and is not resting on the bench.

	What does he wear?	Where is he from?	What is he doing?
Tourist A			
Tourist B			
Tourist C			

Solutions on page 37

The words got lost...

Sort the words according to their numbers. Each set of numbers makes a sentence. Find the sentences

4 the	2 France	7 the	1 what	8 Versailles	3 Paris	8 Palace	4 arch	5 Notre	1 fun	5 Dame
3 is	5 is	8 was	5 one	8 built	6 the	7 Obelisk	8 by	2 is	8 king	7 is
6 Louvre	1 we	4. of	2 located	6 is	7 the	5 of	4 triumph	3 also	8 Louis	5 the
5 most	3 called	8 the	5 famous	6 the	4 commem-orates	3 the	8 14th	7 symbol	1 are	7 of
1 going	4 Napoleon's	2 in	6 biggest	3 city	7 the	4 army's	6 museums	5 cathedrals	3 of	1 to
2 Europe	5 in	6 in	7 Concorde	6 the	4 victory	7 Plaza	5 Europe	1 Paris	6 world	3 lights

1. —————————————————————

2. —————————————————————

3. —————————————————————

4. —————————————————————

5. —————————————————————

6. —————————————————————

7. —————————————————————

8. —————————————————————

Solutions on page 37

Trivia

1. In what continent is France located?

2. True or false - France is the third largest country in Europe?

3. Which natural border separates France, Italy and Switzerland?

4. True or false - The French Alps is the name of a river?

5. What is the French flag called?

6. What colors appear on the French flag?

7. What currency is used in France?

8. True or false - The Arch of Triumph was built by king Louis the 14th.

9. Complete: "If they don't have bread let them eat…"

10. True or false - Napoleon met his death while fighting in a battle for the glory of France?

11. Which famous French king was crowned at the age of five?

12. True or false - Charles de Gaulle was the king who built the Versailles palace?

13. Who built the Versailles palace?

14. What is a patisserie?

15. How do you pronounce "croissant"?

16. What is Tarte Tatin?

17. How do you say good morning in French?

solutions on the next page

Trivia (page 36) **Solutions**

1. Europe
2. True (After Russia and Ukraine)
3. The French Alps
4. False—The name of a mountain range that separates France, Italy and Switzerland.
5. The Tricolor (for the three colors that appear on it).
6. Blue, white and red
7. The Euro
8. False—the Arch of Triumph was build by Napoleon to commemorate his big battle victories.
9. Cake (attributed to Marie Antoinette)
10. False—He died on the island of Saint Helena after he lost at the battle of Waterloo and was exiled from France.
11. King Louis 14th
12. False—Charles de Gaulle was one of the strong people who helped to rebuild France and turn it into a great power.
13. King Loius the 14th
14. A pastry bakery
15. Krwasson
16. A famous French dessert—sort of an upside-down apple pie.
17. Bonjour

Words got lost (page 35)

1. what a fun, we are going to Paris
2. France is located in Europe
3. Paris is also called the City of Lights
4. The arch of triumph commemorates Napoleon's army's victory
5. Notre Dame is one of the most famous cathedrals in Europe
6. The Louvre is the biggest museums in the world
7. The Obelisk is the symbol of the Concorde Plaza
8. Versailles Palace was built by King Louis the 14th

Who am I and what is my name (and what do I do...)? (page 37)

	What does he wear?	Where is he from?	What is he doing?
Tourist A	A jeans	Israel	Taking pictures
Tourist B	A pants and a shirt	USA	resting on the bench
Tourist C	a suit	England	Drink

Coloring pages

L'Arc de Triomphe (the Arch of Triumph)

A journal

date   What did we do?

date   What did we do?

Printed in Germany
by Amazon Distribution
GmbH, Leipzig